LEARN SCIENCE WITH MO

LIGHT AND SHADOWS

I0879021

Paul Mason

Michael Buxton

Enslow PUBLISHING

Published in 2026 by Enslow Publishing, LLC
2544 Clinton Street
Buffalo, NY 14224

First published in Great Britain in 2023 by Wayland
Copyright © Hodder and Stoughton 2023

Editor: John Hort
Design: Collaborate
Illustrations: Michael Buxton
Science consultant: Peter Riley

All rights reserved. No part of this book may be reproduced in any form without permission in writing from the publisher, except by a reviewer.

Manufactured in the United States of America

CPSIA compliance information: Batch #CSENS26: For further information contact Enslow Publishing LLC, New York, New York at 1-800-398-2504.

Please visit our website, www.enslowpublishing.com. For a free color catalog of all our high-quality books, call toll free 1-800-398-2504 or fax 1-877-980-4454.

Cataloging-in-Publication Data
Names: Mason, Paul. | Buxton, Michael, illustrator.
Title: Light and shadows / Paul Mason ; illustrated by Michael Buxton.
Description: Buffalo, NY : Enslow Publishing, 2026. | Series: Learn science with Mo | Includes glossary and index.
Identifiers: ISBN 9781978544727 (pbk.) | ISBN 9781978544734 (library bound) | ISBN 9781978544741 (ebook)
Subjects: LCSH: Light--Juvenile literature. | Shades and shadows--Juvenile literature.
Classification: LCC QC360.M376 2026 | DDC 535.'4--dc23

Find us on

Contents

The words in **bold** are in the glossary on page 30.

Learning about LIGHT

Mo is a little bit afraid of the dark. In fact, sometimes at night Mo gets REALLY scared and hides under the covers.

This does not make sense. It is even darker under the covers than it is outside them!

Perhaps you can help Mo feel braver?
Most things are less frightening if we understand them.

If we learn about light and **shadows**, the darkness might not seem so frightening.

It's easier to remember things when they're fun, so Mo's going to learn about light and shadows on a visit to a funfair while ...

... visiting the Hall of Mirrors ...

... trying to win prizes in Archery Alley ...

... and even visiting the House of Horrors!

LIGHT SOURCES

Mo and Sid set off to the fair on a sunny afternoon. In fact, the sun is SO bright that Mo decides to wear sunglasses.

All light comes from somewhere. Things that produce light are called **light sources**. During the daytime, the sun is our biggest light source.

Which of these are also light sources? The answer is on page 32.

Light sources are not all the same. Some light sources release heat and others do not. The sun, for example, warms the earth – even though it is VERY far away.

The sun is a **natural** light source. It was not made by humans. Other light sources are made by humans. They are called **artificial** light sources.

Mo, try putting these light sources into different groups, according to whether they are natural or artificial. We've done the first two to help you. If you get it right, you've earned your choice of ride at the funfair.

Natural	The sun ? ? ?
Artificial	Candle ? ?

Can you help Mo with this challenge? The answers are on page 32.

BLOCKING LIGHT

To get to the fair, Mo and Sid go down Shady Lane. The trees turn the path into a kind of tunnel. They block out the sunshine.

Shade and shadows are places where light does not reach because it has been blocked. Objects that block all light are **opaque**. Objects that let some light through are **translucent**. Objects that let light through are **transparent**.

Do you know which of these would block the most light (and have the darkest shadow)? Number them one to three, from most to least, and then check your answers on page 32.

Shady Lane is cool as well as dark. This is because heat travels with light from the Sun. When light is blocked, heat is usually blocked too.

Mo, can you separate the light sources from page 7 into hot ones and cool ones?

	Hot	Not Hot
Natural	The sun Log fire Volcano	**Firefly**
Artificial	Candle	Cell phone Flashlight

That's correct, Mo. Add another ride to your funfair visit!

Be careful, sunlight can damage your eyes. Even cool monsters wearing sunglasses should never look straight at the sun.

SHADOW games

When Mo and Sid come out of Shady Lane, it is very sunny. Their shapes are casting huge, scary shadows on the ground.

Shadows move and change if the light source moves.

Mo, which of these pictures shows Sid's shadow in the middle of the day when the sun is high in the sky?

A B C

Correct! When the sun is high in the sky, Sid's shadow is shorter.

Moving the light source is not the only way to make a shadow change. Shadows also change if the object that is blocking the light moves.

Mo, get a strong flashlight in a dark room. Shine the flashlight away from you, so that your hands cast a shadow on the wall.

Now you're going to make a bird fly.

Mo invents some other shadow animals. Can you work out what they are?

(There is one more way to change a shadow ... find out about it on pages 14–15.)

Fun with MIRRORS

When Mo and Sid arrive at the fair, the sun has started to go down. The fair has turned on the lights. There are light sources everywhere!

Outside the Hall of **Mirrors** is a normal mirror.

Take a look at your **reflection**, Mo. You're looking good!

Mo, you're holding your sunglasses in your right hand aren't you? But do you notice anything strange in the mirror?

Let's find out what's going on ...

Reflection is how we see things that are not light sources. Light bounces off them and into our eyes.

Light bounces off the mirror and into Mo's eyes. A mirror image is like a friend facing you. If they raise their right arm, it is on YOUR left. (You could do this as an experiment, to check.)

Mirror image

Photograph

Mirror images look different from photographs. Those just show what a friend looking at you would see.

Correct!

RAINBOW Shadows

Mo and Sid are standing in front of one of the stalls when they notice something strange. Their shadows are no longer dark grey. They are colored!

It does look a bit like a rainbow, Sid. Rainbows contain the different colors that make up light.

The most important colors are reds, greens and blues. Mixing them together in different ways can make over a million different colors.

Mo can do an **experiment** to find out.

Mo uses some flashlights with colored plastic over the lenses. He also needs a white card to shine them on, and a dark room.

Mo puts the red flashlight in between the other two and shines all three on the same part of the white card. What color is the middle bit of light Mo?

Now Mo holds a pencil in between the flashlights and the card (close to the card usually works best). He can see three different colored shadows!

The different colored lights come from different directions. The pencil blocks some of them out. The "shadows" are made up of the colors that have not been blocked.

LIGHT RAYS

Mo has spotted a stall called **Archery** Alley. To win a prize, you have to hit the **bullseye** with your arrow. One of the cuddly toy prizes looks just like Sid!

Mo, can you see the target clearly? If you can, what's the science explanation?

Correct!

Now, what path does the light take from the target to your eye?

We can do an **experiment** to find out. Mo will need three pieces of cardstock with holes in the middle, some putty to hold them up, a flashlight, and a dark room.

1. Shine the flashlight along a tabletop, so that the light goes through the hole in the first card.

2. Now line up the second and third cards so that you can see the light through all three holes.

What kind of line goes between the three holes?

Correct. So now we know that light travels in straight lines!

To check this, move the middle card a bit aside. Can you still see the light?

MIRROR tricks

Next, Mo and Sid decide they'd like to visit the Hall of Mirrors. The mirror outside shows both of them looking just like normal.

When we look in a mirror, our brains think we are seeing something that is actually there. We think the light is bouncing off an object and into our eyes. The odd-shaped mirrors in the Hall of Mirrors, though, fool our brains.

Adding lines to a drawing of a mirror that bulges out will help you to understand, Mo.

1. Light travels from the object to the mirror.

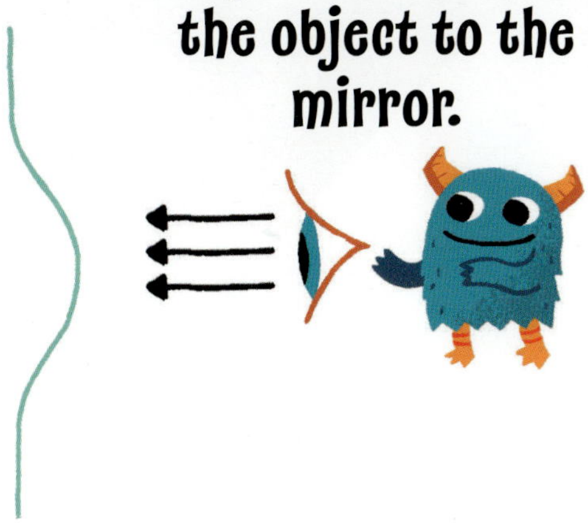

2. When light bounces off the curve it is spread out.

3. The brain can't understand the image as it usually does. It is fooled into thinking the object is shorter.

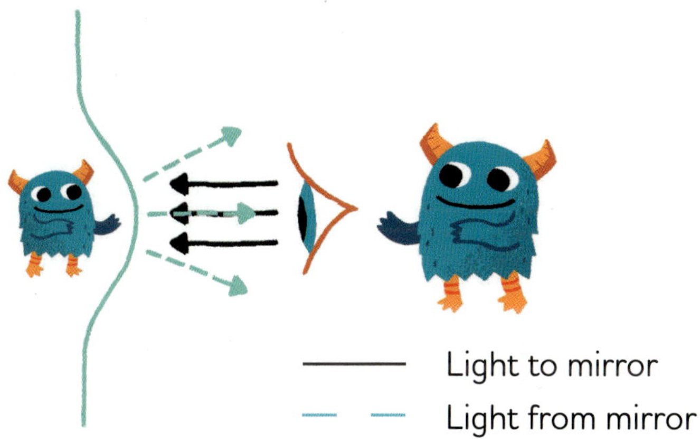

The changing MOON

While Mo and Sid were in the Hall of Mirrors, it got dark. There is still light to see, though, because the moon has come up. Tonight, the moon is a circle shape.

The moon's light comes from the sun. The sun's light travels across space, hits the moon and bounces back to Earth, where we see it as moonlight.

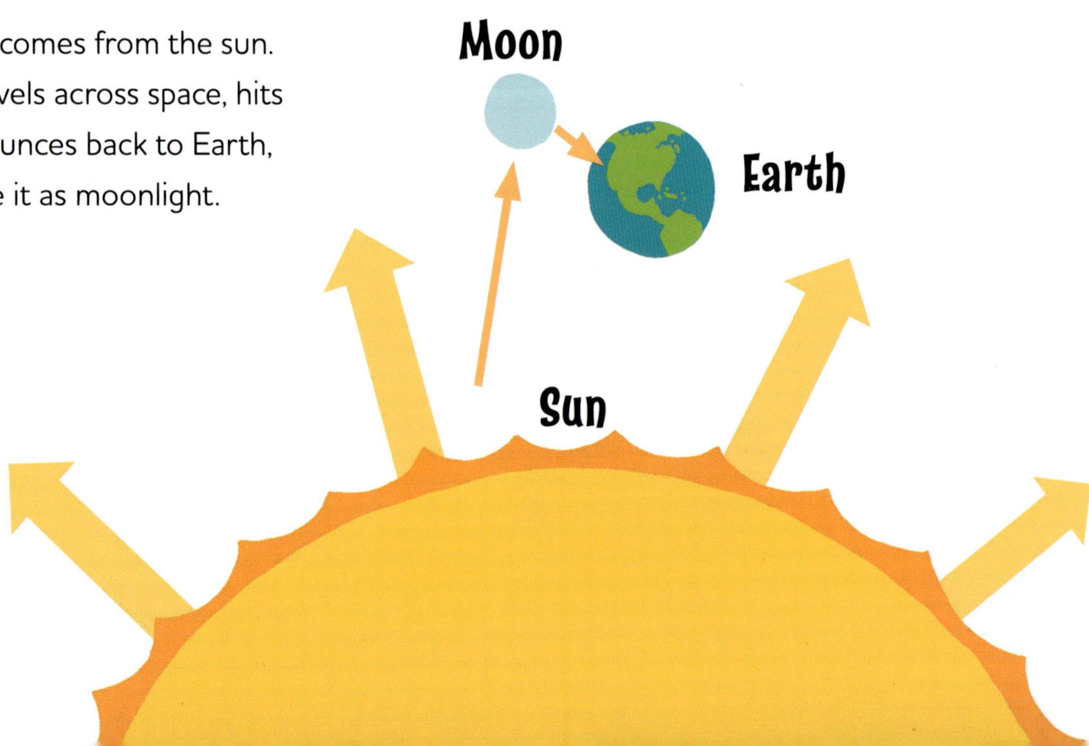

The moon looks like a different shape at different times of the month. Mo, can you guess why?

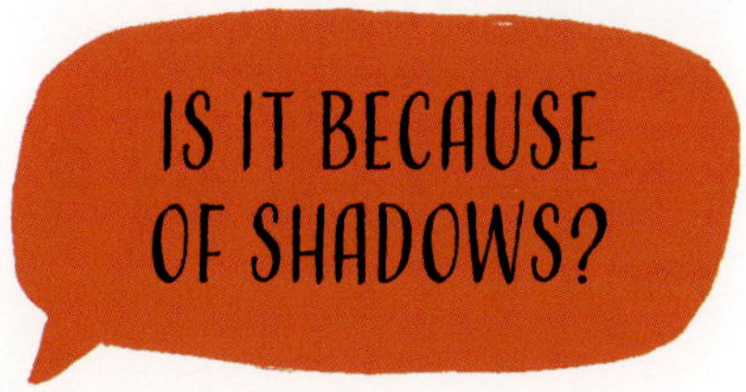

Correct! Let's see how it happens.

The sun is always shining at the moon. The half of the moon facing the sun is always lit up. The other half is always in shadow.

The moon travels around and around the earth. The same side always faces the earth.

New Moon

The moon is between the sun and the earth and blocks the sunlight. We see the shadowed side and so see no moon.

Last-quarter Moon

We see half of the moon lit and the other half in shadow.

Full Moon

The moon moves to where all the side facing Earth is lit up, and we see a full moon.

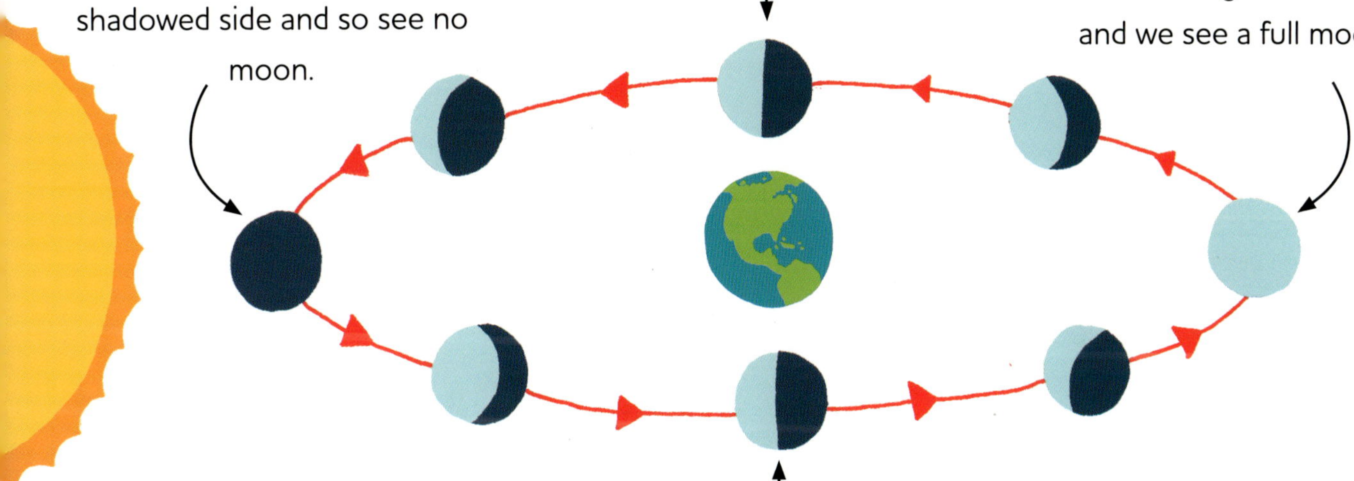

First-quarter Moon

The moon moves so there is less shadow and we come to see half of its surface in light.

Big and small SHADOWS

The next stall Mo wants to visit is the puppet show. Here, the Wolf puppet has some sausages ... and the Crocodile wants them.

The Crocodile needs to scare the Wolf by making his shadow look as big and scary as possible.

The size of a shadow depends on how close the light source is to the object that is blocking it.

Close to the light source you cast a big shadow.

Further from the light source you cast a smaller shadow.

A long way from the light source, your shadow is not very big or scary at all.

Mo, shall we help the Crocodile scare the Wolf into giving up the sausages?

THAT'S IT! START FAR AWAY FROM THE LIGHT.

NOW COME CLOSER TO THE LIGHT.

NOW COME MUCH CLOSER.

Did the Crocodile share his sausages with you, Mo?

LIGHT AND SENSES

Our eyes help our brains work out what is happening in the world around us. Our brains use information from other senses, too.

Our sense of smell helps us eat fresh food ...

Without light to see with, our brains sometimes make mistakes about the world around us. This is why the dark can be scary. Unless we can see, noises in the dark could be something creeping up on us.

Next, Mo is visiting the House of Horrors. It will be a scared-of-the-dark training session, to test how brave Mo is when he cannot see.

Mo has to touch and feel things he can't see. When the lights come on, Mo will see if he was right to be scared.

A-MAZE-ZING LIGHT TRICKS

It is nearly time to go home. Before they leave, Mo and Sid have time for one last stall. They are going into the Amazing Maze.

The maze is really hard to find your way through.

There are doorways that aren't doorways:

Can you explain how the maze used light to fool you, Mo?

That's correct.

The painting fooled your brain in the same way as the mirror on page 19.

Correct!

HAPPY IN THE DARK

When the two friends leave the fair, it has gotten completely dark. Sid has a flashlight for the dark parts, but even with that Mo would usually be scared. Have the lessons about light helped Mo feel safer?

Mo, what direction does Sid need to point the flashlight to see the path?

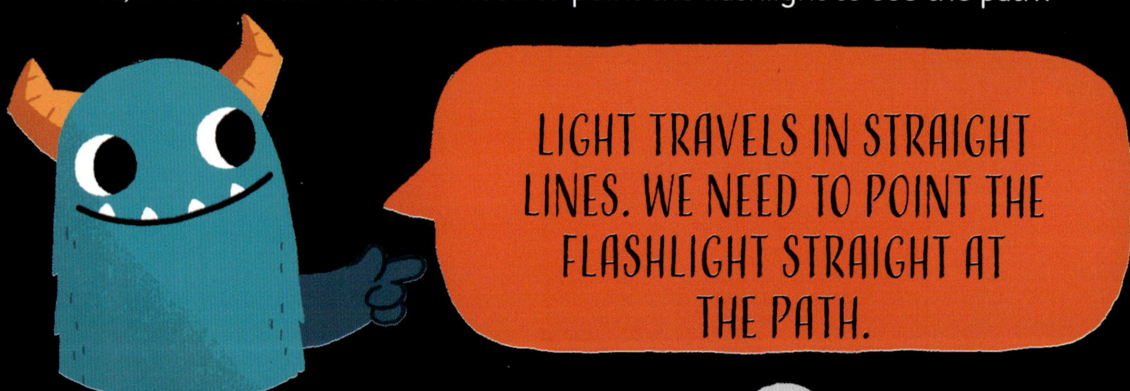

Mo, how did you know?
I KNEW THE MOON WAS SHINING LIGHT ON US.
THE TREE WAS BETWEEN THE MOON AND THE PATH.
SO THE SHAPE ON THE PATH WAS THE SHADOW FROM THE TREE.
Is there someone behind us?
NO, DON'T WORRY.
Mo, how did you know THAT?
I JUST LOOKED AT THE REFLECTION IN THE WINDOW. IT SHOWED ME THERE WAS NOTHING FOLLOWING US.
Mo, are you still scared of the dark?
HMM ... NOT REALLY!

Glossary

archery
using a bow and arrow

artificial
material that is made by humans, rather than growing naturally. For example, plastic, glass, and metal are all artificial.

bullseye
middle part of a target

experiment
test to see what happens

firefly
small insect with a body that can send light signals in the dark. Their name is not very accurate: fireflies are actually beetles, and only the males can fly.

light source
object that produces light, for example a flashlight, candle, lightbulb, phone screen, or the sun

mirror
object that reflects light well enough for someone to see a clear picture in it. Mirrors are usually made of glass with a silvery material behind it.

natural
material that is made by nature, instead of by humans. For example, wood, sand and water are all natural.

opaque
an object that blocks all light and cannot be seen through

reflection
light bouncing back from an object. "Reflection" is also used to describe the image we see in a mirror and other smooth, shiny objects.

shadow
place where light does not reach because it has been blocked

translucent
an object that blocks some light so things behind it can be seen, but not very clearly

transparent
an object that does not block light and can be seen through

Books to read

Quick Fix Science: Light by Paul Mason (Wayland, 2021)

Meet Snappy, a young Nile crocodile. Snappy is really interested in science, but not all that good at it yet. In this book, Snappy finds out about light, what it is and how it works.

Spectacular Light and Sound by Rob Colson and Jon Richards (Gareth Stevens Publishing, 2024)

Attention-grabbing facts and explanations about extreme forms of light and sound, from the loudest bangs to the kind of light that lets you look inside a human body.

Why Does a Mirror Show Things Back to Front? And Other Questions About Light by Anna Claybourne (Wayland, 2020)

This book has the answers to many of your questions about light, mirrors, more!

Places to visit

Exploratorium
Pier 15, San Francisco, CA, 94111

The museum has displays showing many different kinds of science in action! Discover more facts about light and shadow and about different activites to try at home..

The Strong National Museum of Play
One Manhattan Square, Rochester, New York, 14607

This is a fantastic museum aimed completely at young visitors. You can do your own experiments, play educational games, and learn more about different kinds of science.

Answers

Page 6

Candle	✓
Balloon	x
Mobile phone	✓
Log fire	✓
Mirror	x
Flashlight	✓
Volcano	✓

Page 7

Natural	The Sun Log fire Volcano Firefly
Artificial	Candle Mobile phone Flashlight

Page 8

1. Brick walls do not let through any light.

2. A cotton sheet would let through some light.

3. A window would let through nearly all the light.